Draw Fashionable Manga Girls

Draw Fashionable Manga Girls
First Published in 2021 by Zakka Workshop, a division of
World Book Media, LLC

www.zakkaworkshop.com
134 Federal Street
Salem, MA 01970 USA
info@zakkaworkshop.com

IDOL WO KAKOU!
Copyright ©2015 Tomomi Mizuna. All rights reserved.
Original Japanese edition published by MAAR-SHA Publishing Co., Ltd.
English language licensed by World Book Media LLC, USA via Tuttle-Mori Agency, Inc., Tokyo, Japan.

Publisher: Taeko Tagami
Design: Seichi Sato (teaspoon)
Editors: Ayako Ogura (teaspoon) and Hiromo Sakurada (Maar-sha)
Translator: Mayumi Anzai
English Editor: Lindsay Fair

ISBN: 978-1-940552-54-5

Printed in China

10 9 8 7 6 5

An Anime Drawing Workbook for Beginners

Draw Fashionable Manga Girls

Tomomi Mizuna

CONTENTS

WHAT YOU'LL NEED

You don't need a lot of fancy art supplies to draw fashionable manga girls. Just grab a pencil and get started using the practice pages in this book. Here are some other tools that you might find helpful:

Drawing paper or a notebook

Tracing paper (transparent paper)

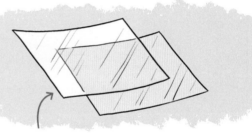

Optional: Use tracing paper for extra practice.

Eraser

Pencil

Colored pencils

Crayons

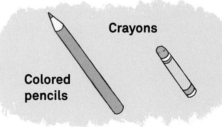

COLORING OPTIONS

If you'd like to add color to your drawings, try using crayons, colored pencils, pens, or watercolor paint. The finished look of your drawing will vary based on what you use to color it. Try out the different options and choose the one that works best for you!

Colored pencil

Start out by lightly coloring the entire illustration. Then go back and add more color to areas you want to make darker.

Crayon

Hold your crayons gently and color lightly for best results.

Pen

Start out by making diagonal strokes in one direction. Then go back and add diagonal strokes in the opposite direction for a crosshatch effect.

Watercolor

Paint the main areas of the drawing first. Once the paint has dried, go back and finish the small, detailed areas, such as accessories.

MANGA DRAWING TECHNIQUES FOR BEGINNERS

Are you new to drawing manga? Then this is the perfect book for you! First, you'll start out by tracing the example illustration, then you'll try your hand at completing the same illustration using the guidelines provided in the book. This learning technique will have you drawing your own manga illustrations in no time!

STEP 1: TRACE

Start out by tracing over the example illustration to practice the style and movements of manga drawings. This is a popular method for learning how to draw manga in Japan.

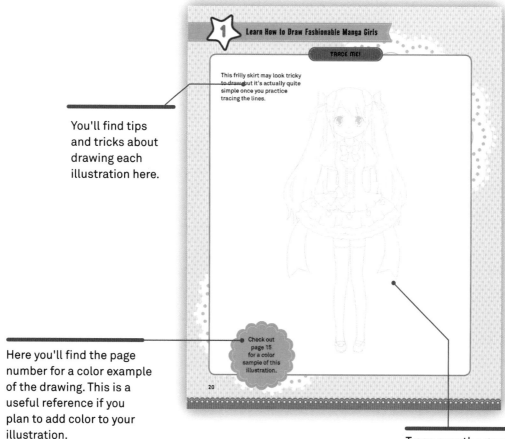

1   Learn How to Draw Fashionable Manga Girls

TRACE ME!

This frilly skirt may look tricky to draw, but it's actually quite simple once you practice tracing the lines.

You'll find tips and tricks about drawing each illustration here.

Check out page 15 for a color sample of this illustration.

20

Here you'll find the page number for a color example of the drawing. This is a useful reference if you plan to add color to your illustration.

Trace over the gray lines.

STEP 2: DRAW

Once you've practiced tracing, it's time to try drawing the illustration! Use the provided guidelines as a foundation for your drawing—they will help you achieve the correct proportions. Experiment by changing the facial expression or style of clothing to make the illustration your own.

You'll find exercises to practice drawing specific elements of the illustration, such as the face.

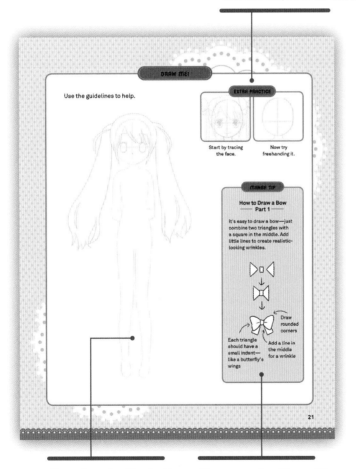

Complete the illustration by drawing on top of the guidelines.

There are also Manga Tips with helpful information and more advanced techniques.

MEET THE FASHIONABLE MANGA GIRLS

In this section, you'll meet a few of my favorite fashionable manga girls, then learn how to draw them yourself! Let's get started!

THE GIRLY GIRL

PROFILE

Name: Momo Ichino

Birthday: July 25th, Leo

Personality: Always cheerful

Best Quality: Laughs often

Likes: Eating sweets

Dislikes: Waking up early

Favorite Animal: Rabbits

My favorite color is pink!

Practice drawing on page 20.

Practice drawing on page 22.

THE COOL CHICK

PROFILE

Name: Aoka Sora

Birthday: May 3rd, Taurus

Personality: Always calm

Best Quality: Good student

Likes: Ice skating

Dislikes: Spicy food

Favorite Animal: Dogs

I love sports!

Practice drawing on page 26.

Practice drawing on page 24.

THE FREE SPIRIT

PROFILE

Name: Lemon Kizawa
Birthday: June 18th, Gemini
Personality: Lots of energy
Best Quality: Artistic
Likes: Ice cream
Dislikes: Caterpillars
Favorite Animal: Hamsters

I love making my own clothes!

Practice drawing on page 30.

Practice drawing on page 28.

THE MUSICIAN

I love that song!

Practice drawing on page 34.

Practice drawing on page 32.

THE LEADER

I love dancing!

Practice drawing on page 38.

Practice drawing on page 36.

TRACE ME!

This frilly skirt may look tricky to draw, but it's actually quite simple once you practice tracing the lines.

Check out page 15 for a color sample of this illustration.

Use the guidelines to help.

Start by tracing the face.

Now try freehanding it.

MANGA TIP

How to Draw a Bow
— Part 1 —

It's easy to draw a bow—just combine two triangles with a square in the middle. Add little lines to create realistic-looking wrinkles.

Draw rounded corners

Each triangle should have a small indent—like a butterfly's wings

Add a line in the middle for a wrinkle

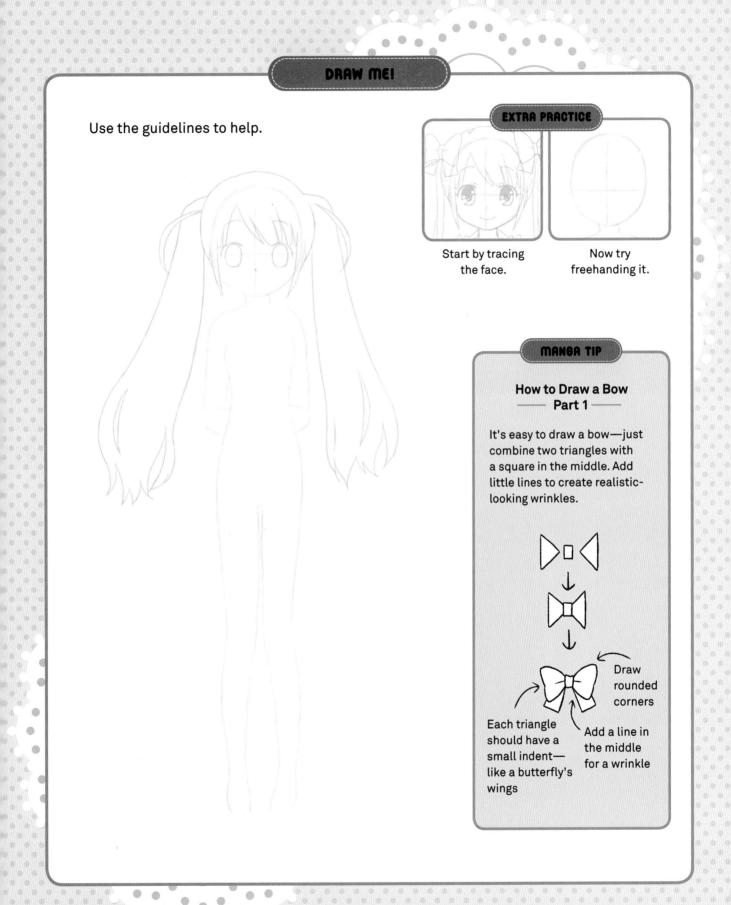

This girly girl loves bows—she's wearing them from head to toe! Pay attention to the way the ribbons twist as she moves.

Check out page 15 for a color sample of this illustration.

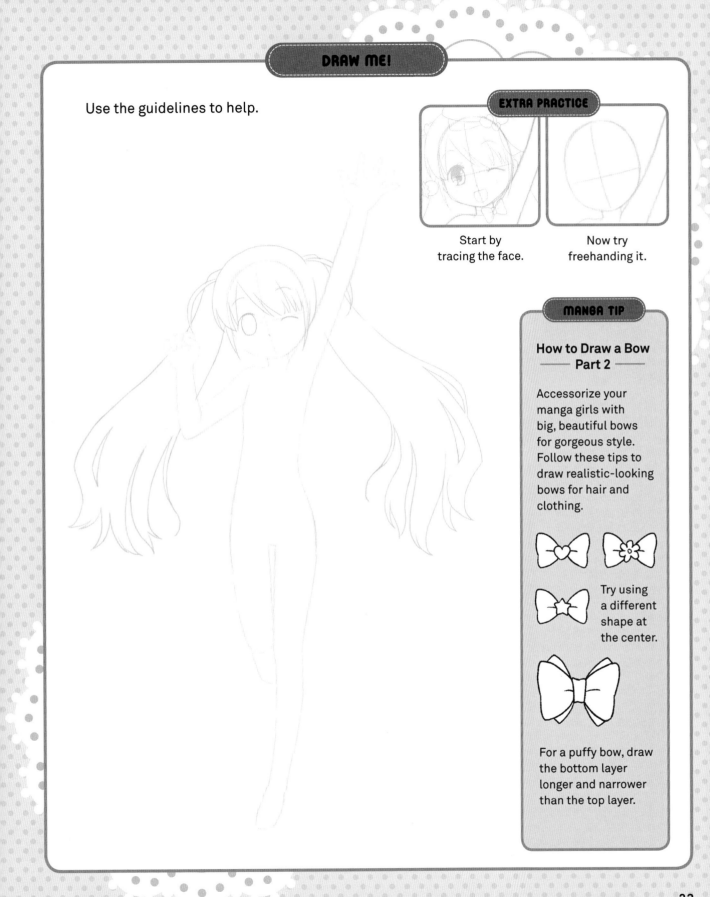

DRAW ME!

Use the guidelines to help.

EXTRA PRACTICE

Start by tracing the face.

Now try freehanding it.

MANGA TIP

How to Draw a Bow
— Part 2 —

Accessorize your manga girls with big, beautiful bows for gorgeous style. Follow these tips to draw realistic-looking bows for hair and clothing.

Try using a different shape at the center.

For a puffy bow, draw the bottom layer longer and narrower than the top layer.

Use diagonal lines to create this puffy, layered skirt. Change the direction of the diamond charms hanging from the skirt hem to show the movement of the wind.

Check out page 16 for a color sample of this illustration.

Use the guidelines to help.

Start by
tracing the face.

Now try
freehanding it.

MANGA TIP

How to Draw the Skirt

To draw the skirt, start by
drawing the wavy outline
of each layer. Next, add
vertical lines for the folds
that form in the fabric. Don't
forget to draw the shadowy
areas where the inside of
the fabric is visible.

1. Wavy outline

2. Draw lines for
the fabric folds

Inside of the fabric

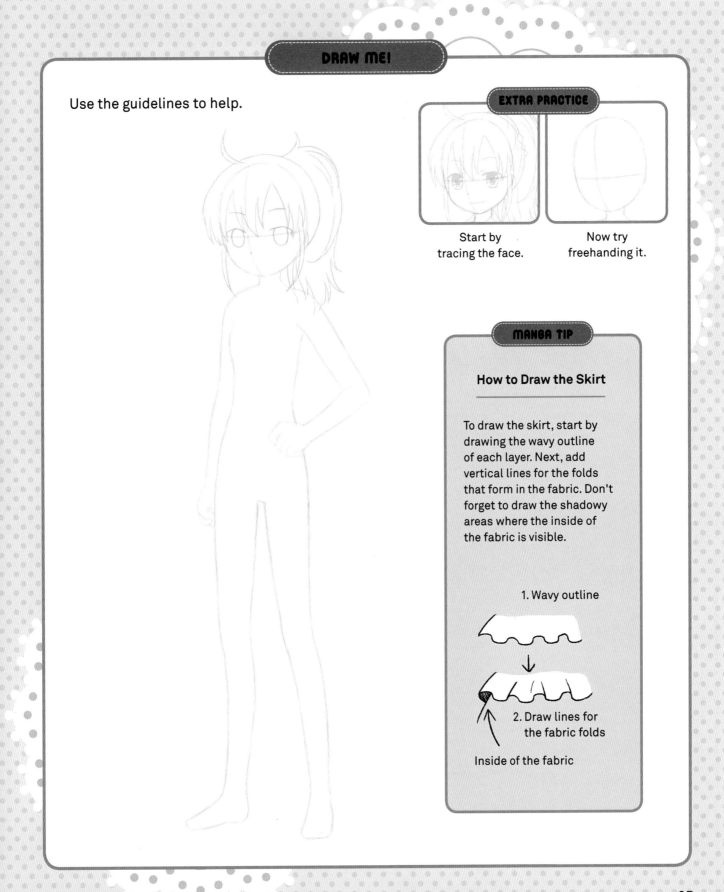

A few special details, such as ribbons, bows, and diamond embellishments, transform this simple dress into a glamorous outfit.

Check out page 16 for a color sample of this illustration.

Use the guidelines to help.

Start by tracing the face.

Now try freehanding it.

MANGA TIP

How to Draw a Bow
— Part 3 —

Even when drawing a simple knot, make sure to add lines for wrinkles in the fabric.

Draw lines for wrinkles

How to Draw a Pleated Skirt

It's important to draw the bottom lines of the pleats in a staggered pattern—just like a staircase.

Draw each pleat staggered

✔ ☐☐☐☐☐ **DO**

✘ ☐☐☐☐☐ **DON'T**

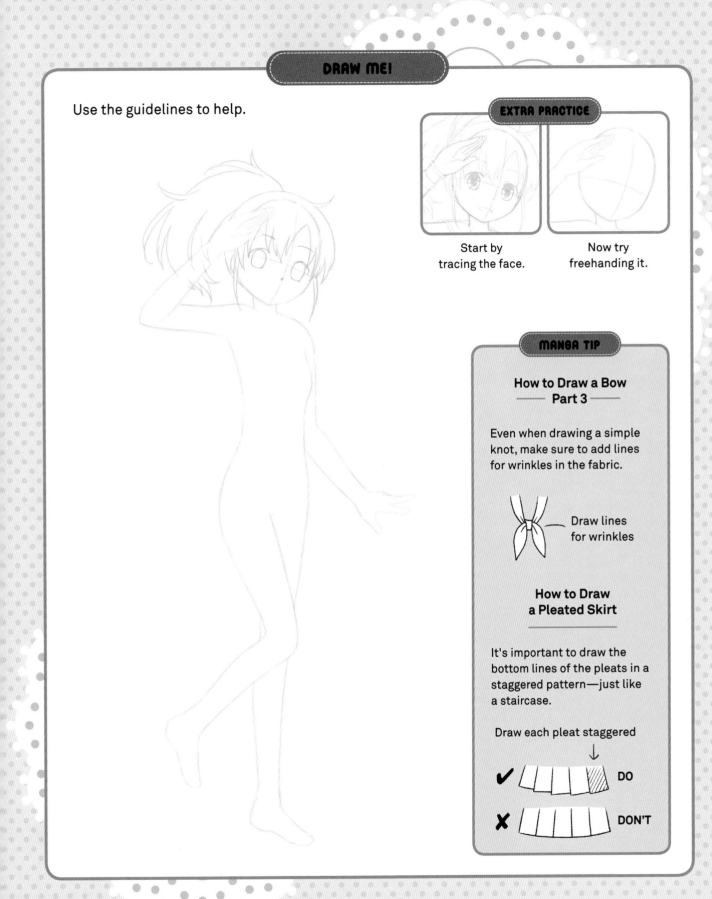

This free spirit isn't afraid to show off her unique personality! Her hair is styled in two donut-inspired buns with open space at the center.

Check out page 17 for a color sample of this illustration.

Use the guidelines to help.

Start by
tracing the face.

Now try
freehanding it.

MANGA TIP

**How to Draw
Striped Socks**

When drawing striped
socks or tights, use
curved lines that
follow the shape of
the leg. Don't use
straight lines!

DON'T   DO

✗   ✔

Draw curved stripes,
not straight ones

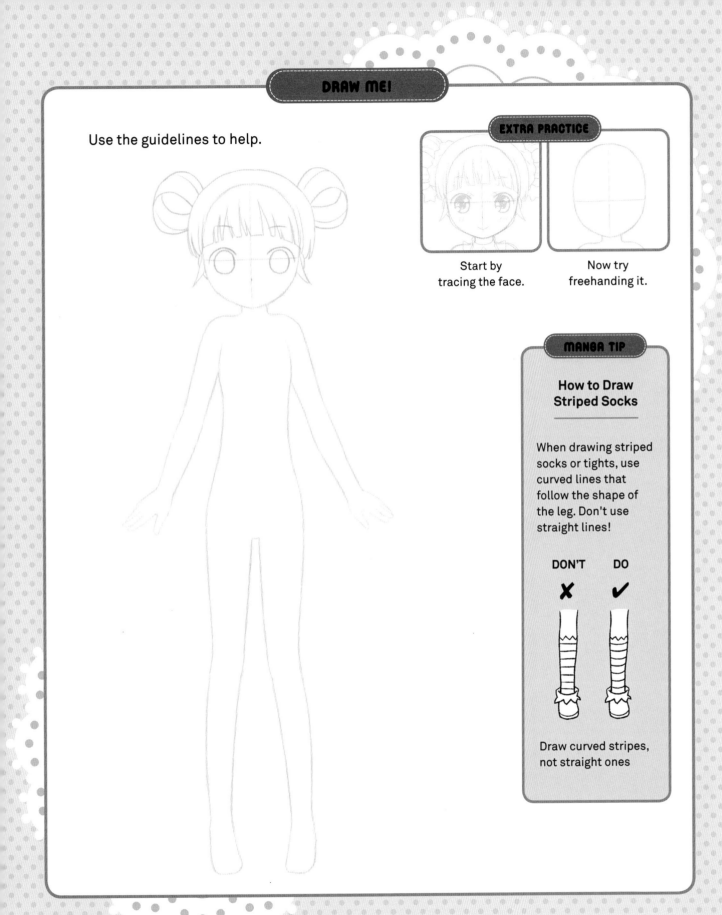

Combine pompoms of different sizes, colors, and patterns for a funky outfit. Top with a variety of ribbons, jewelry, and other accessories for added flair.

Check out page 17 for a color sample of this illustration.

Use the guidelines to help.

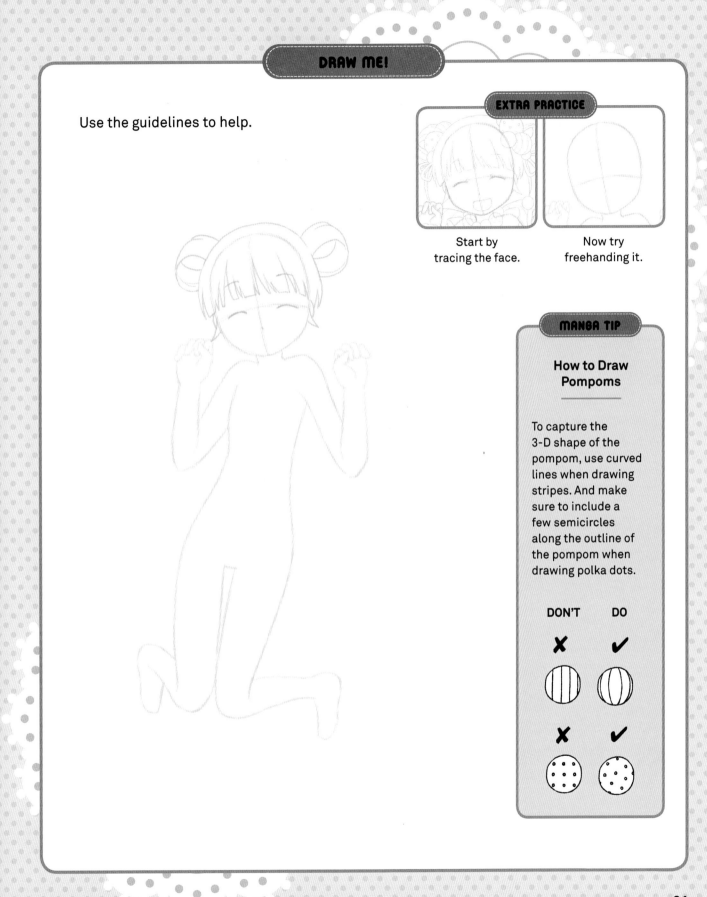

Start by
tracing the face.

Now try
freehanding it.

MANGA TIP

How to Draw Pompoms

To capture the
3-D shape of the
pompom, use curved
lines when drawing
stripes. And make
sure to include a
few semicircles
along the outline of
the pompom when
drawing polka dots.

DON'T   DO

✗   ✔

✗   ✔

This gothic-style outfit features sleeves and a collar shaped like bat wings. Use dark, moody shades when coloring this design.

Check out page 18 for a color sample of this illustration.

Use the guidelines to help.

Start by
tracing the face.

Now try
freehanding it.

MANGA TIP

How to Draw a Frilly Skirt

There are two important
elements to drawing a
frilly skirt. First, use wavy
lines to draw the different
tiers. Next, combine short
and long vertical lines to
capture the wrinkles that
form in the fabric.

← Short line

← Long line

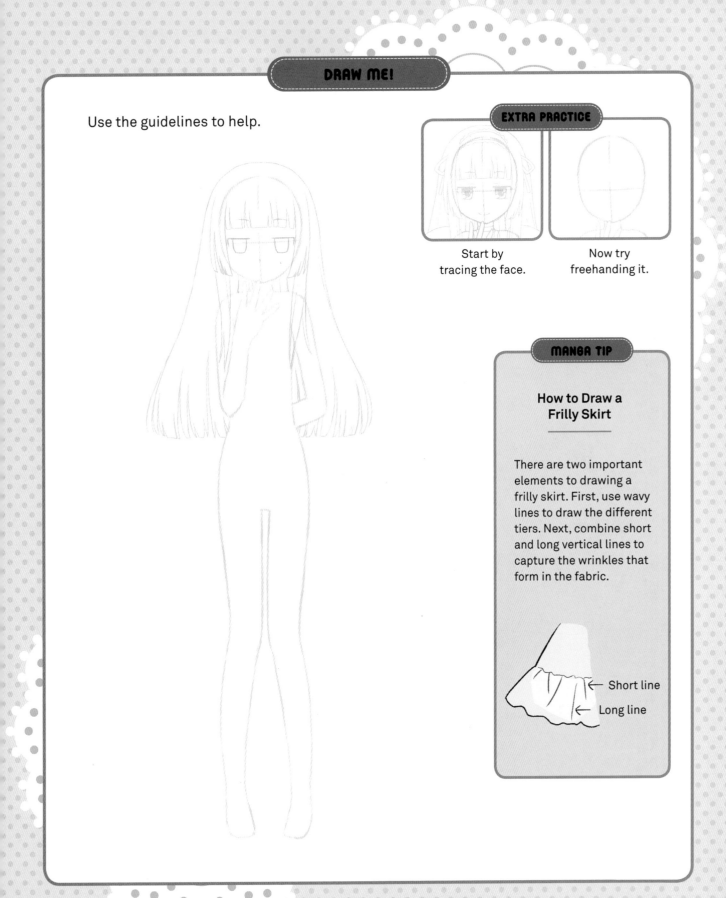

This outfit is designed for a music lover. It features both music notes and a piano key skirt.

Check out page 18 for a color sample of this illustration.

Use the guidelines to help.

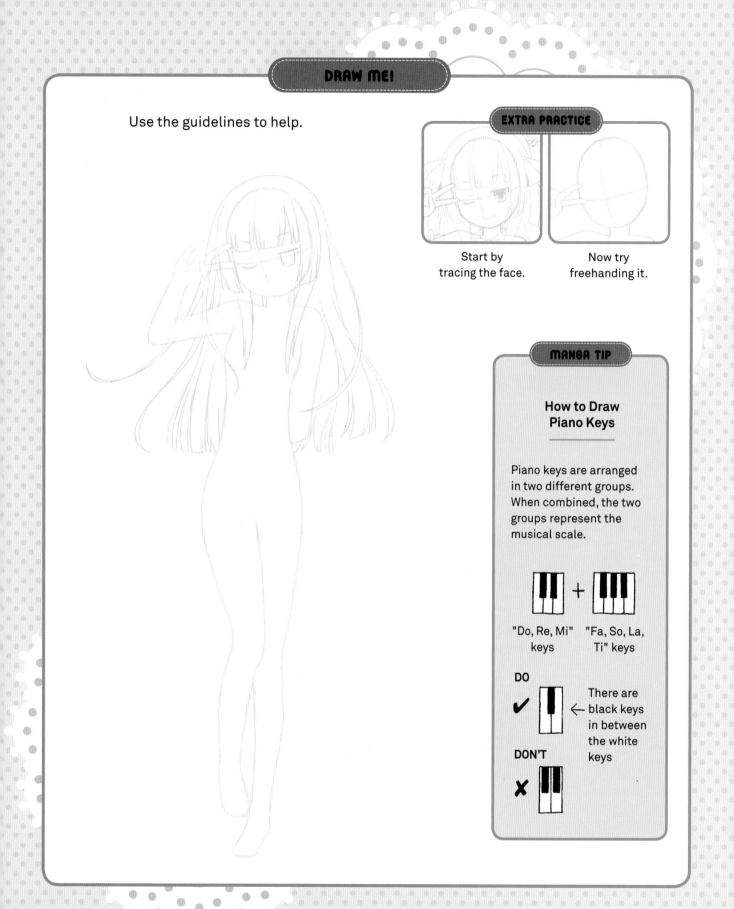

Start by
tracing the face.

Now try
freehanding it.

MANGA TIP

How to Draw Piano Keys

Piano keys are arranged in two different groups. When combined, the two groups represent the musical scale.

+

"Do, Re, Mi" keys

"Fa, So, La, Ti" keys

DO

✔

← There are black keys in between the white keys

DON'T

✗

Practice tracing the hair and spiral shaped curls. Notice how the curls get smaller at the ends.

Check out page 19 for a color sample of this illustration.

Use the guidelines to help.

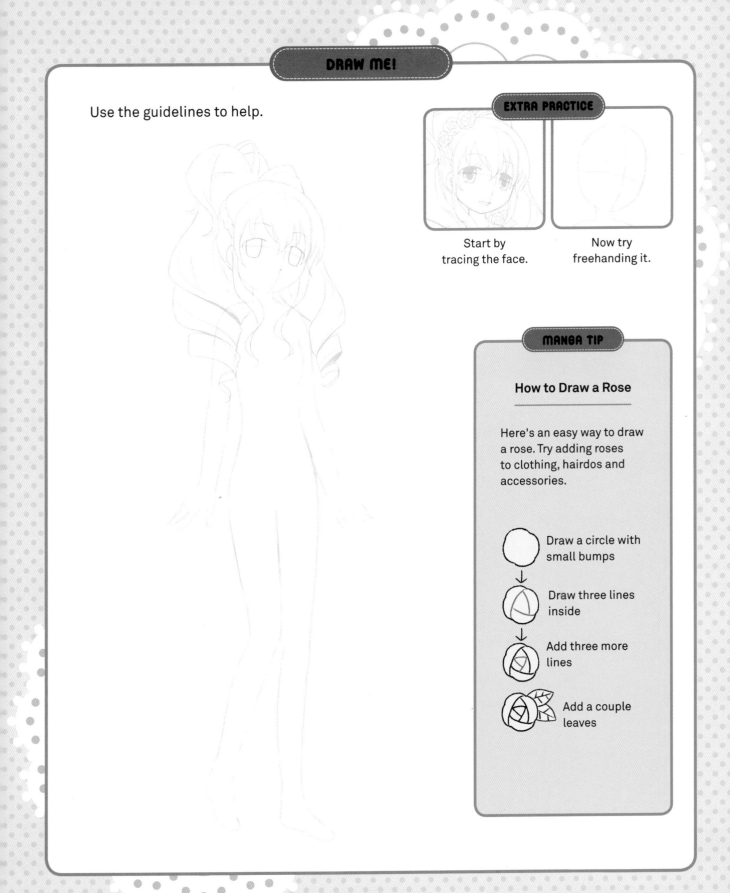

Start by
tracing the face.

Now try
freehanding it.

MANGA TIP

How to Draw a Rose

Here's an easy way to draw
a rose. Try adding roses
to clothing, hairdos and
accessories.

Draw a circle with
small bumps

Draw three lines
inside

Add three more
lines

Add a couple
leaves

Try drawing a skirt with lots of ruffles for a dramatic look. Don't forget that the inside of the skirt will be visible in certain spots when she moves.

Check out page 19 for a color sample of this illustration.

Use the guidelines to help.

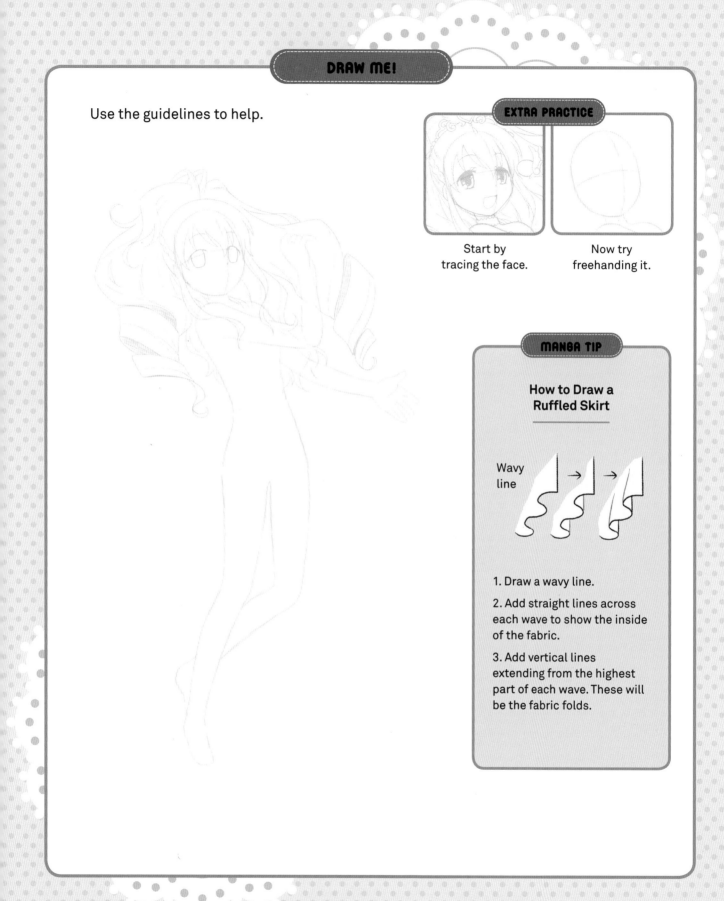

Start by tracing the face.

Now try freehanding it.

MANGA TIP

How to Draw a Ruffled Skirt

Wavy line

1. Draw a wavy line.

2. Add straight lines across each wave to show the inside of the fabric.

3. Add vertical lines extending from the highest part of each wave. These will be the fabric folds.

PATTERNS

Patterns are a simple way to add personality to an outfit. Here you'll find some pattern inspiration for your fashionable manga girls. Mix and match your favorites to create a fun outfit.

Checks

Try changing the width and orientation of the lines.

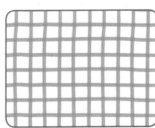
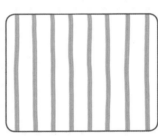
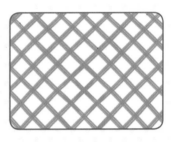

Stripes

Vary the width and orientation of the lines— try horizontal, vertical, and diagonal!

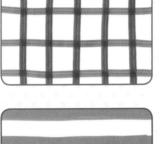

Dots

Change the size or change the amount of space between the dots.

Shapes

Design your own pattern using a variety of different shapes.

Lines

These designs look great along the hem of a skirt or sleeve.

Lines
Stripes

Dots
Shapes

Checks
Stripes

Stripes
Lines
Dots

Color me using your favorite patterns!

THEMES

When designing your own fashionable manga girls, select a motif or theme for your character. Incorporate this theme into the different parts of her outfit, such as her hair, clothing, and accessories. Let's get creative!

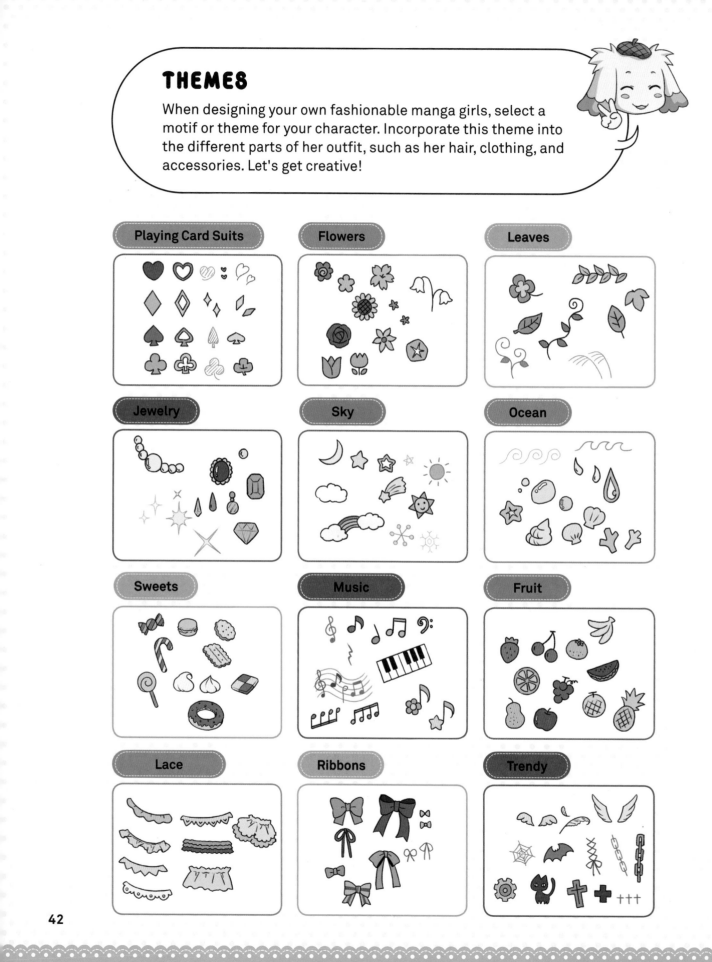

Playing Card Suits

Flowers

Leaves

Jewelry

Sky

Ocean

Sweets

Music

Fruit

Lace

Ribbons

Trendy

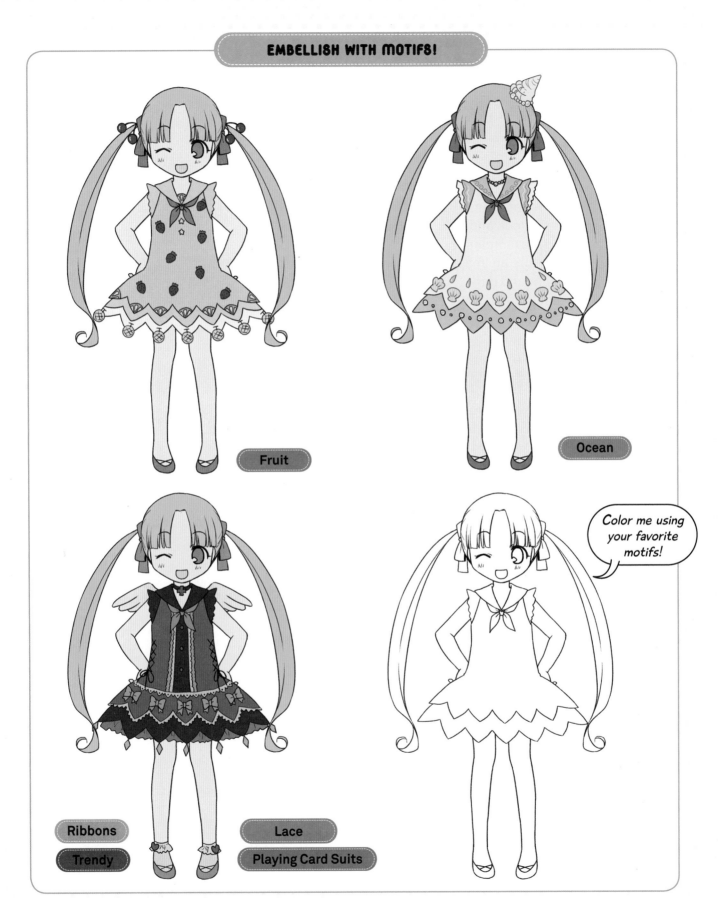

COLOR SCHEMES

Using different colors can change the entire look and feel of a drawing. The examples on this page feature an image colored with light and dark shades of a single color, while the examples on page 45 feature an image colored with a variety of different hues. Have fun experimenting with different colors to create the desired effect.

Red

Passionate and bold

Blue

Quiet and refreshing

Yellow

Energetic and cheerful

Green

Natural and kind

Purple

Elegant and mature

Bright

Pastel

Funky

Refreshing

Sweet

Practice Pages

Now take what you've learned about patterns and color combinations to create stylish outfits for these fashionable manga girls!

SCALE & SILHOUETTE

Changing the length of a skirt or the shape of a sleeve can have a big impact on the finished design. It's important to think about scale and silhouette when drawing clothes.

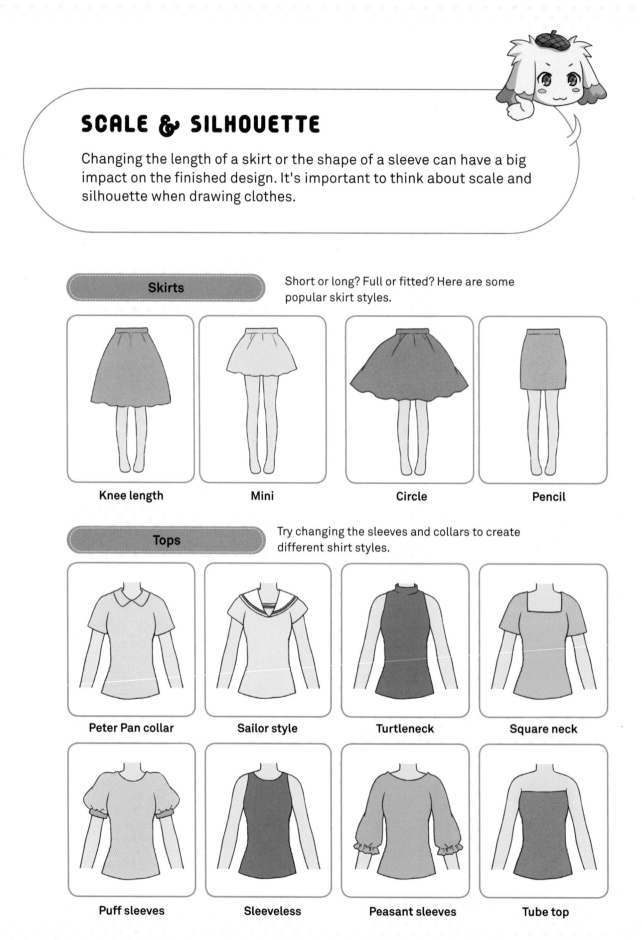

Skirts

Short or long? Full or fitted? Here are some popular skirt styles.

Knee length

Mini

Circle

Pencil

Tops

Try changing the sleeves and collars to create different shirt styles.

Peter Pan collar

Sailor style

Turtleneck

Square neck

Puff sleeves

Sleeveless

Peasant sleeves

Tube top

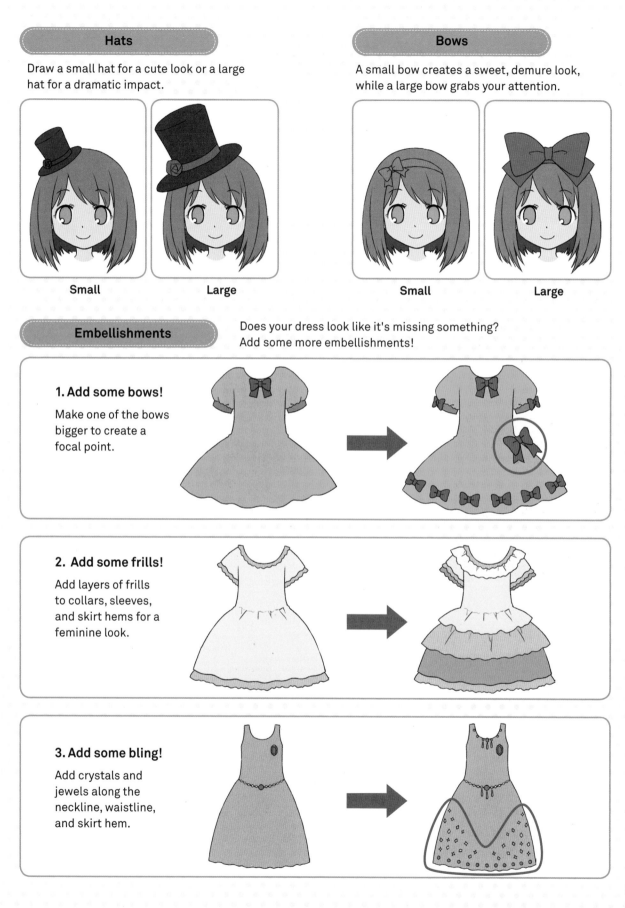

Hats

Draw a small hat for a cute look or a large hat for a dramatic impact.

Small

Large

Bows

A small bow creates a sweet, demure look, while a large bow grabs your attention.

Small

Large

Embellishments

Does your dress look like it's missing something? Add some more embellishments!

1. Add some bows!

Make one of the bows bigger to create a focal point.

2. Add some frills!

Add layers of frills to collars, sleeves, and skirt hems for a feminine look.

3. Add some bling!

Add crystals and jewels along the neckline, waistline, and skirt hem.

HAIRSTYLES & ACCESSORIES

Use these hairstyles to complete the drawings on practice pages 54-55. You may want to copy them onto tracing paper, then practice drawing them on your own. Once you've mastered it, select your favorites to design your own fashionable manga girls!

Hairstyles

Long

Princess cut

Curls

Curly low pigtails

Long and wavy

Long side ponytail

Side ponytail

Short bob

Long bob

Loose, low pigtails

Pigtails

Low pigtails

Loose side ponytail

High ponytail

Messy pigtails

Spiky side ponytail

Short bob with bangs

Buns

Newsboy cap

Headband with bow

Head scarf

Bows

Hat

Barrettes

Cloth headband

Flower crown

Beret

Pillbox hat

Microphone headset

Microphone headset

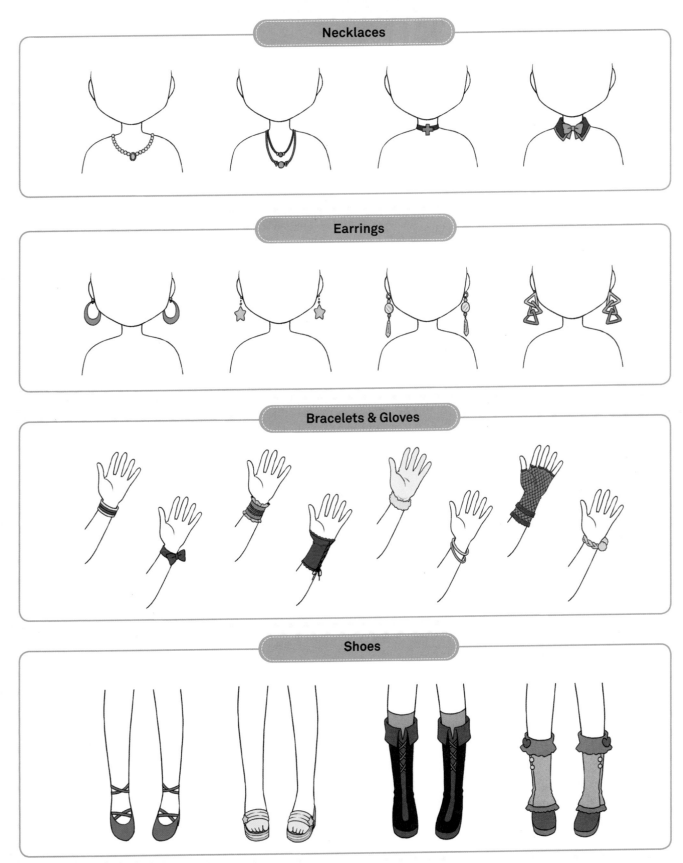

Now try drawing some of your own hairstyles and accessories!

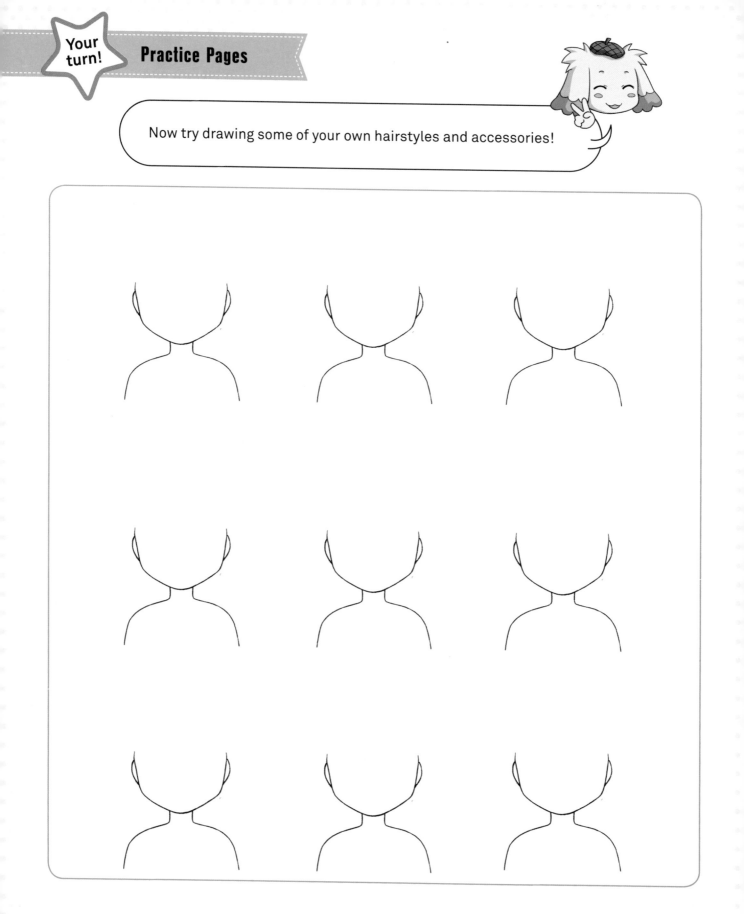

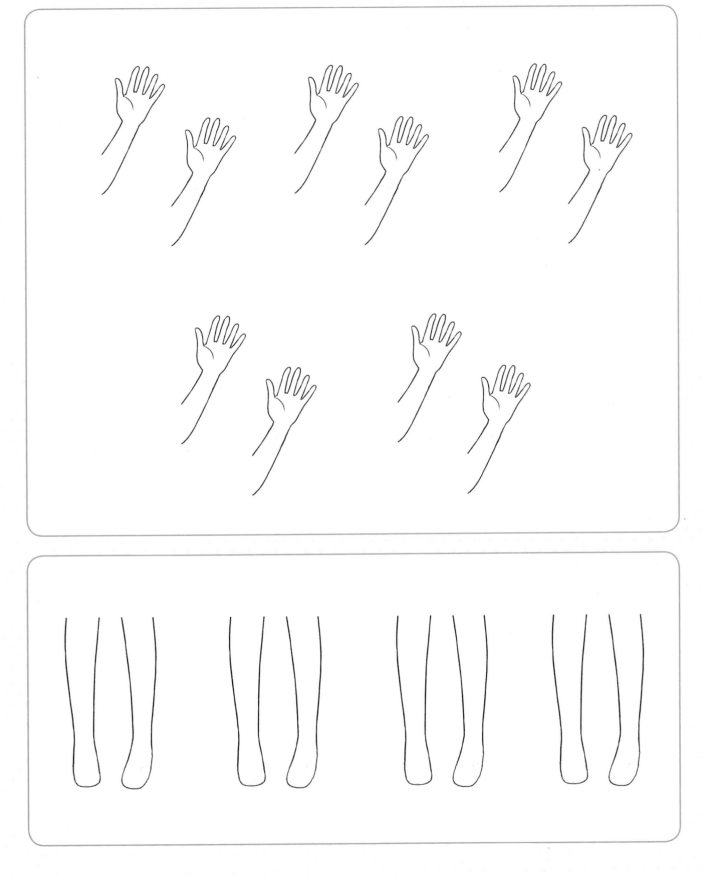

DESIGN YOUR OWN FASHIONABLE MANGA GIRLS

1. Select a hairstyle (refer to pages 50-51).

2. Draw the clothes incorporating color and pattern (refer to pages 40-45).

Hmm...

I did it!

3. Add some accessories to complete the outfit (refer to pages 52-53).

Now it's your turn to design your own fashionable manga girls! Follow the instructions on the opposite page to add hairstyles, clothing, and accessories to these blank forms.

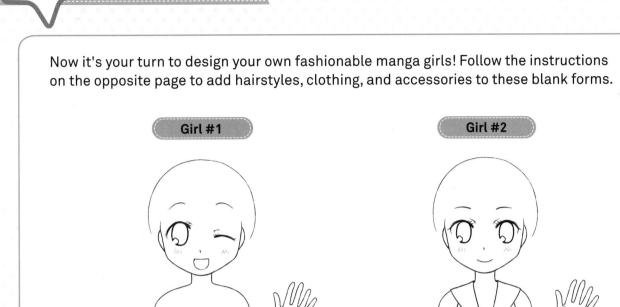

Girl #1

Girl #2

Girl #1

Girl #2

Girl #1

Girl #2

HOW TO DRAW FACES

Now let's learn how to draw faces so you can create your own fashionable manga girls. You'll use guidelines to learn where to position the eyes and mouth.

FRONT VIEW

Eyes

Make sure that both eyes are aligned. When closed, the eyes should be just below the horizontal guideline.

Hair

Draw the hair slightly outside the guideline for the head. This will create volume.

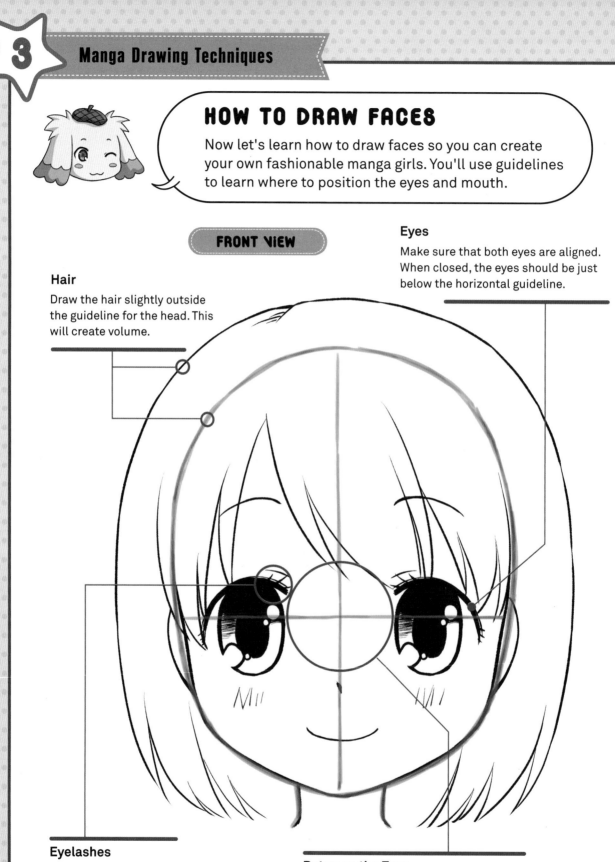

Eyelashes

Add a few eyelashes for a feminine look.

Between the Eyes

For the classic manga look, position the eyes wide. There should be space for another eye in between.

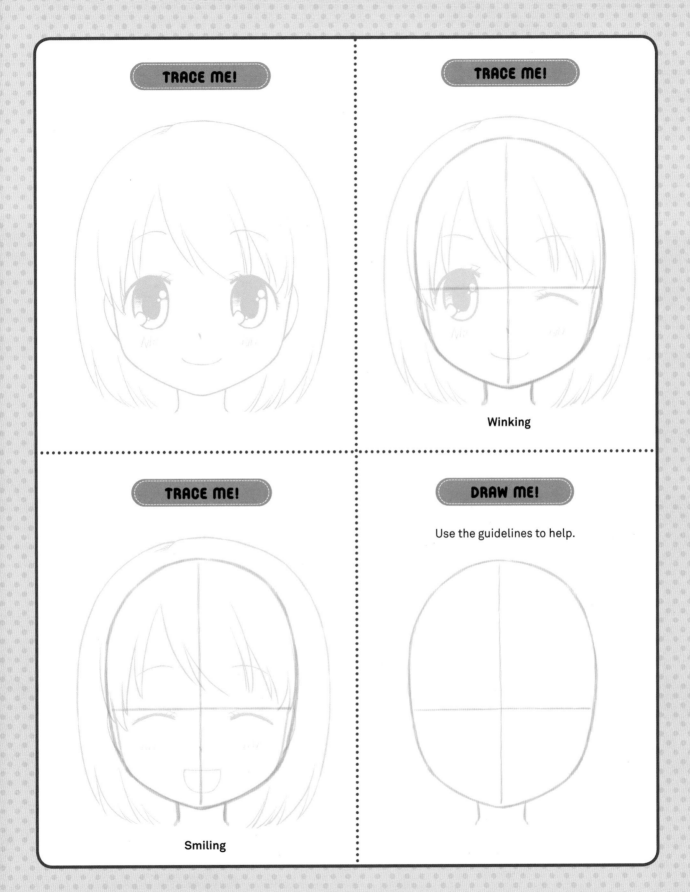

TRACE ME!

TRACE ME!

Winking

TRACE ME!

Smiling

DRAW ME!

Use the guidelines to help.

Drawing a profile, or side view of the face, is a bit more challenging, but you'll be fine as long as you use the guidelines!

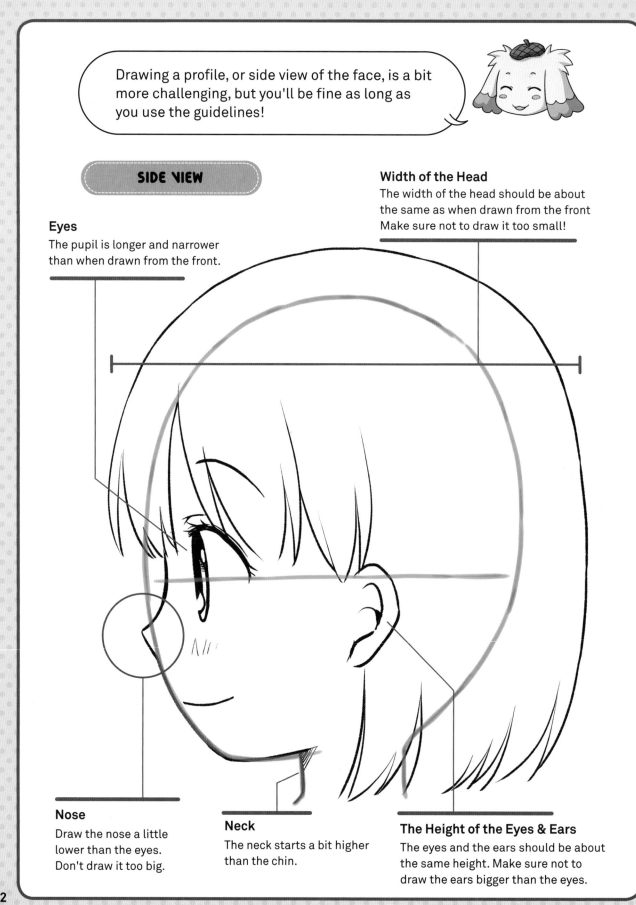

SIDE VIEW

Width of the Head
The width of the head should be about the same as when drawn from the front Make sure not to draw it too small!

Eyes
The pupil is longer and narrower than when drawn from the front.

Nose
Draw the nose a little lower than the eyes. Don't draw it too big.

Neck
The neck starts a bit higher than the chin.

The Height of the Eyes & Ears
The eyes and the ears should be about the same height. Make sure not to draw the ears bigger than the eyes.

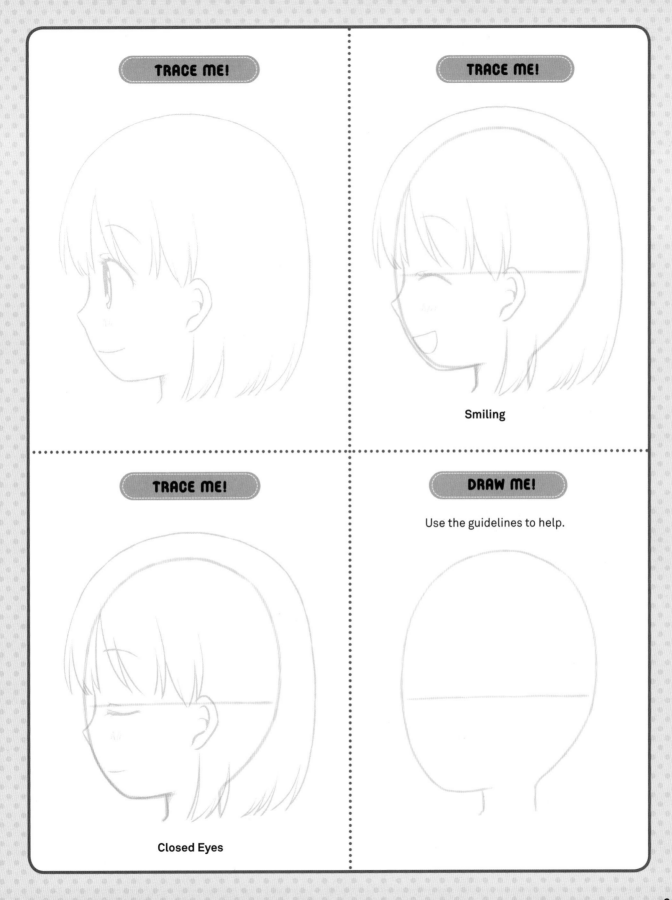

TRACE ME!

TRACE ME!

Smiling

TRACE ME!

DRAW ME!

Use the guidelines to help.

Closed Eyes

HOW TO DRAW FACIAL EXPRESSIONS

It's important to be able to draw different facial expressions to show the emotions of your fashionable manga girls. Here, we'll learn how to change the facial features to show common expressions.

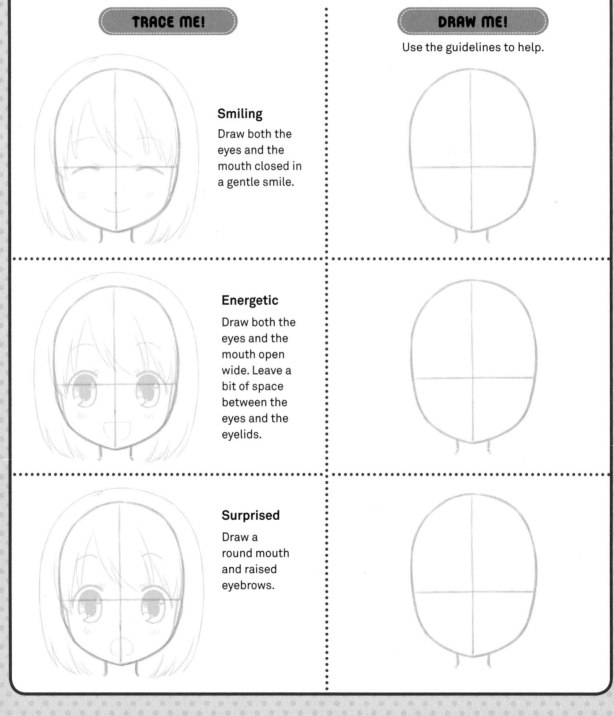

TRACE ME!

DRAW ME!

Use the guidelines to help.

Smiling

Draw both the eyes and the mouth closed in a gentle smile.

Energetic

Draw both the eyes and the mouth open wide. Leave a bit of space between the eyes and the eyelids.

Surprised

Draw a round mouth and raised eyebrows.

Crying

Draw the eyes using sideways V shapes and add tears streaming from the corners.

Weeping

For a less intense crying expression, lower the ends of the eyebrows and draw large teardrops at the corners of the eyes.

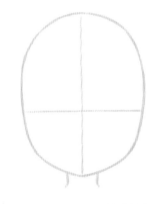

Annoyed

Draw the eyes a little narrower by lowering the eyelids. Raise the ends of the eyebrows and lower the corners of the mouth in a frown.

Worried

Lower the ends of the eyebrows and use a wavy shape to draw the mouth.

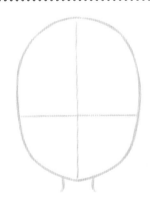

HOW TO DRAW EYES

The eyes are the windows to the soul. Here we'll learn how to draw large eyes full of emotion.

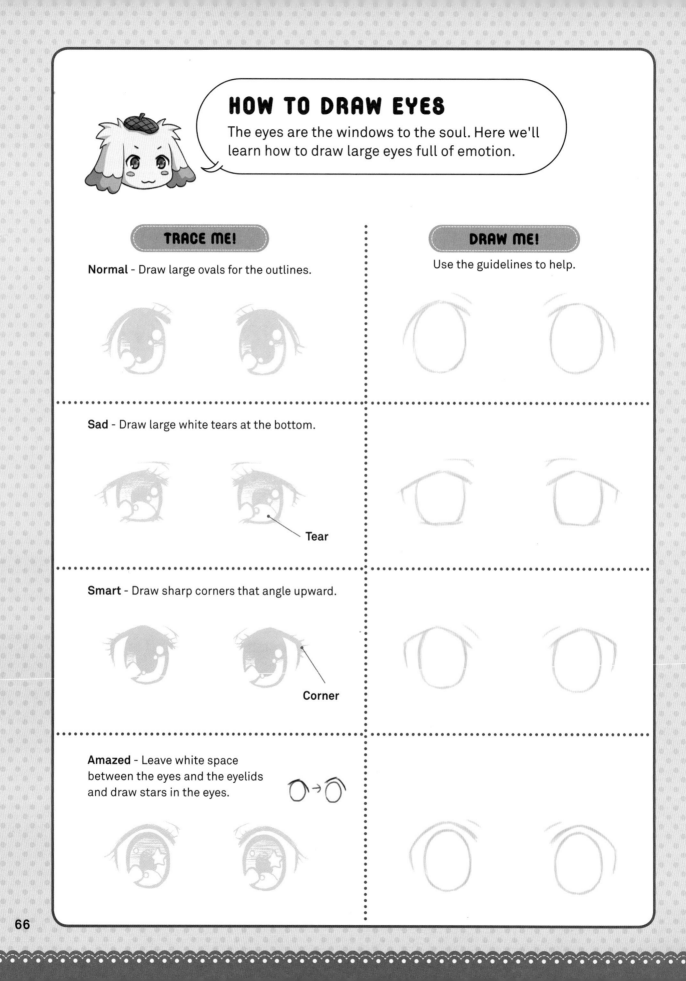

TRACE ME!

Normal - Draw large ovals for the outlines.

Sad - Draw large white tears at the bottom.

Tear

Smart - Draw sharp corners that angle upward.

Corner

Amazed - Leave white space between the eyes and the eyelids and draw stars in the eyes.

DRAW ME!

Use the guidelines to help.

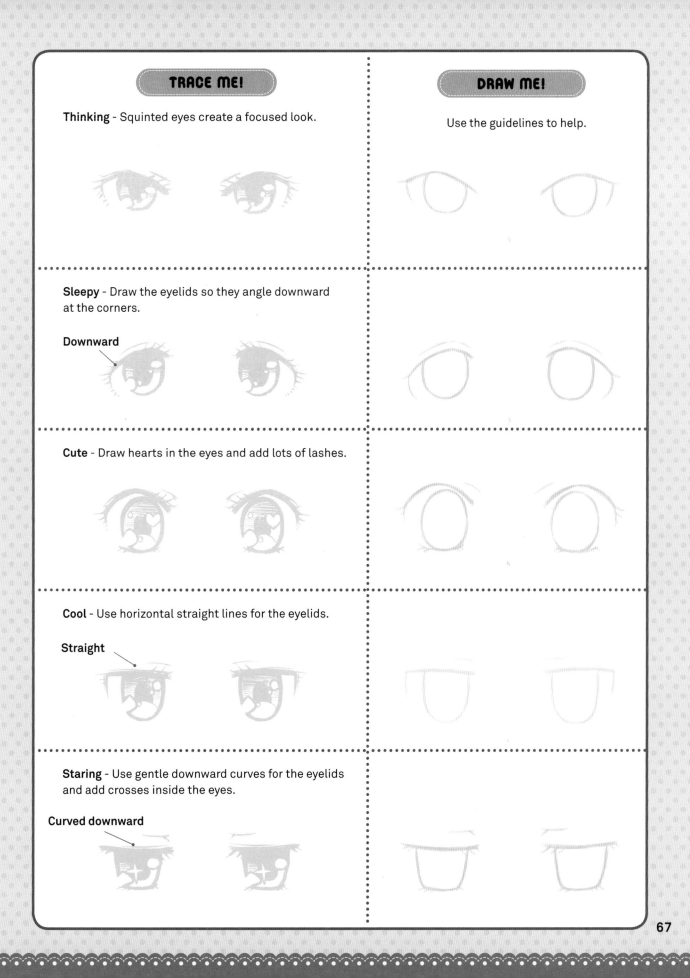

Thinking - Squinted eyes create a focused look.

Use the guidelines to help.

Sleepy - Draw the eyelids so they angle downward at the corners.

Downward

Cute - Draw hearts in the eyes and add lots of lashes.

Cool - Use horizontal straight lines for the eyelids.

Straight

Staring - Use gentle downward curves for the eyelids and add crosses inside the eyes.

Curved downward

Practice Pages

Now try drawing some more facial expressions using what you've learned!

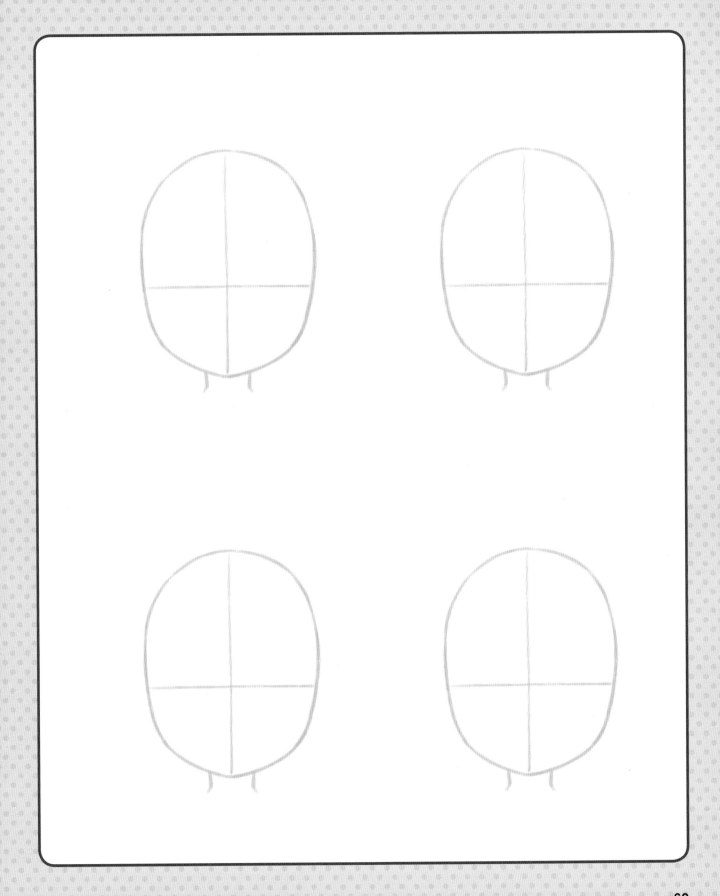

HOW TO DRAW BODIES

Don't be intimidated to draw bodies for your manga girls. The secret is to use the correct proportions to create balanced drawings. As a general rule, the body should be about 5-6 times longer than the head.

TRACE ME!

Front

DRAW ME!

Use the guidelines to help.

Rule #1
The length from the neck to the waist is about the same size as the head.

Rule #2
The legs should be about three times as long as the head.

TRACE ME!

Side

DRAW ME!

Use the guidelines to help.

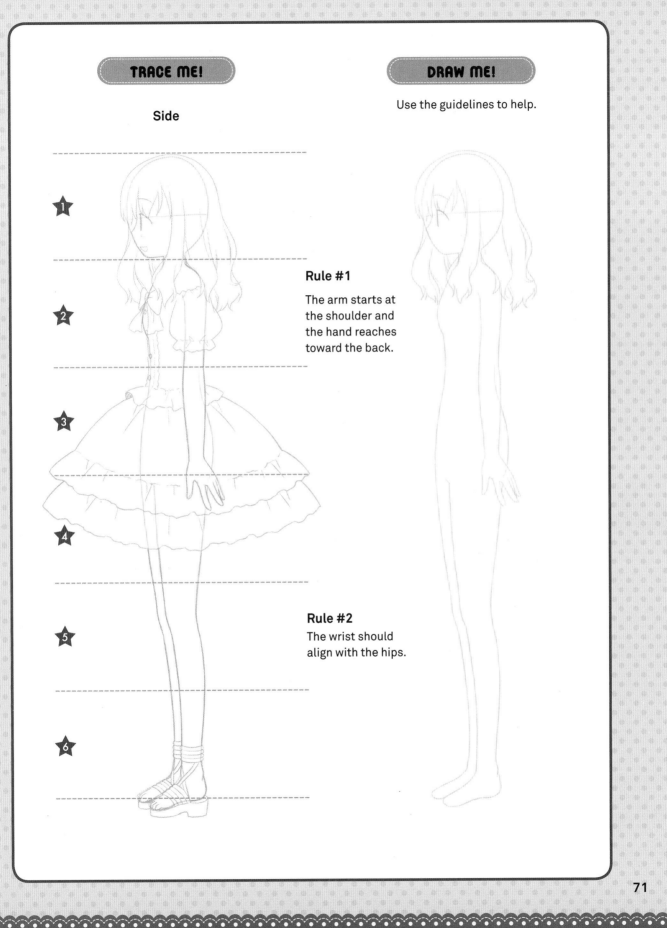

⭐ 1

⭐ 2

Rule #1

The arm starts at
the shoulder and
the hand reaches
toward the back.

⭐ 3

⭐ 4

Rule #2

The wrist should
align with the hips.

⭐ 5

⭐ 6

HOW TO DRAW HANDS

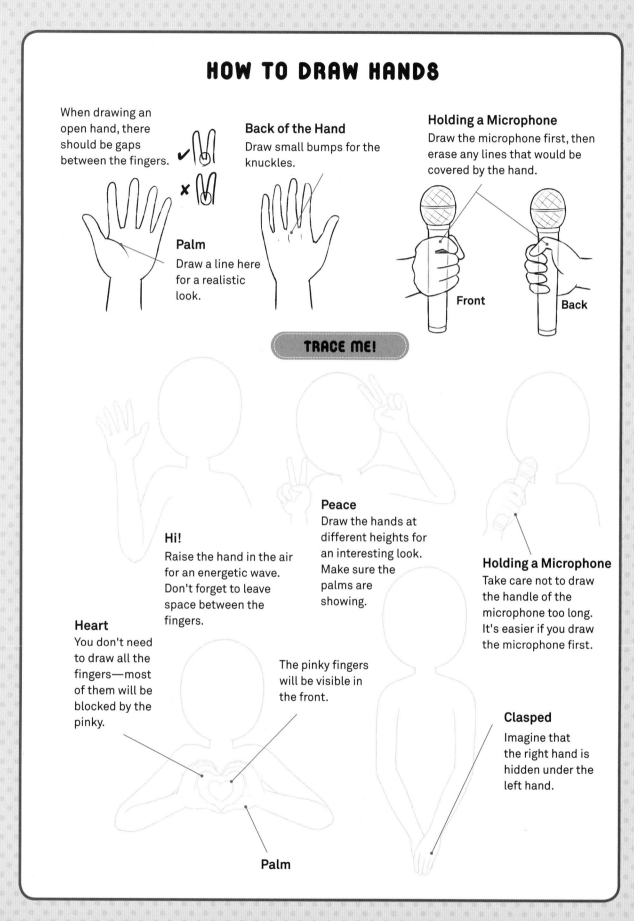

When drawing an open hand, there should be gaps between the fingers.

Back of the Hand
Draw small bumps for the knuckles.

Holding a Microphone
Draw the microphone first, then erase any lines that would be covered by the hand.

Palm
Draw a line here for a realistic look.

Front

Back

TRACE ME!

Hi!
Raise the hand in the air for an energetic wave. Don't forget to leave space between the fingers.

Peace
Draw the hands at different heights for an interesting look. Make sure the palms are showing.

Holding a Microphone
Take care not to draw the handle of the microphone too long. It's easier if you draw the microphone first.

Heart
You don't need to draw all the fingers—most of them will be blocked by the pinky.

The pinky fingers will be visible in the front.

Clasped
Imagine that the right hand is hidden under the left hand.

Palm

HOW TO DRAW LEGS

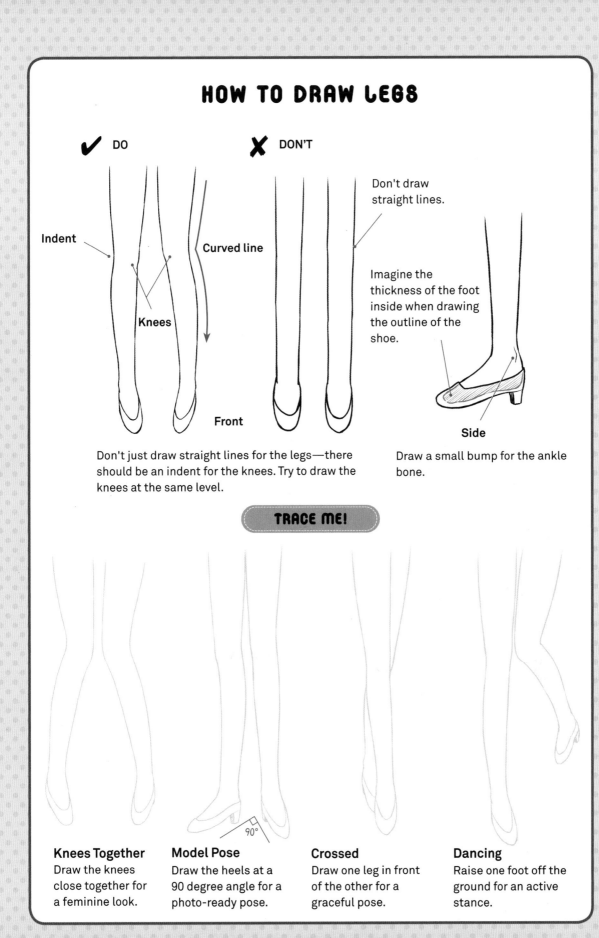

✔ DO   ✗ DON'T

Indent

Curved line

Knees

Front

Don't draw straight lines.

Imagine the thickness of the foot inside when drawing the outline of the shoe.

Side

Don't just draw straight lines for the legs—there should be an indent for the knees. Try to draw the knees at the same level.

Draw a small bump for the ankle bone.

TRACE ME!

Knees Together
Draw the knees close together for a feminine look.

Model Pose
Draw the heels at a 90 degree angle for a photo-ready pose.

90°

Crossed
Draw one leg in front of the other for a graceful pose.

Dancing
Raise one foot off the ground for an active stance.

DRAW YOUR FASHIONABLE MANGA GIRL

It helps to think about your character's personality before you start drawing. That way, you can incorporate unique details into her outfit and facial expression.

I did it! I drew my own fashionable manga girl!

Oh, let me see!

Ta da!

She's so cute! Great job! Now tell me all about her.

Her name is Ruby. She loves singing and dancing and her favorite color is pink.

Cool!

Now, it's your turn!

Who will you draw?

Use these pages to draw your own fashionable manga girls and fill in the profiles.

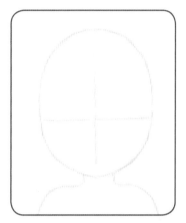

Name:

Age:

Birthday:

Nickname:

All About Her Clothes:

Personality:

Favorite Thing:

Now draw your own fashionable manga girls and fill in the profiles!

Name:

Age:

Birthday:

Nickname:

All About Her Clothes:

Personality:

Favorite Thing:

Name:

Age:

Birthday:

Nickname:

All About Her Clothes:

Personality:

Favorite Thing:

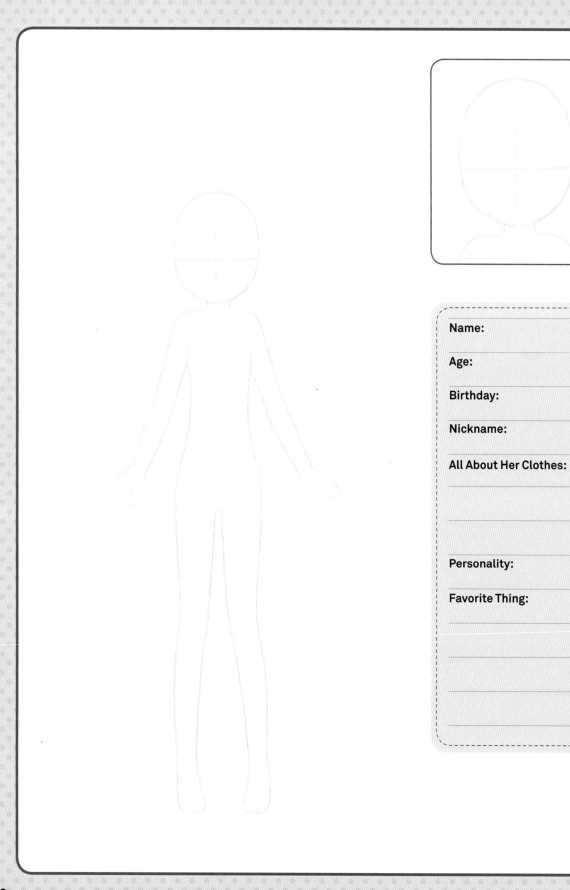

Name:

Age:

Birthday:

Nickname:

All About Her Clothes:

Personality:

Favorite Thing:

Name:

Age:

Birthday:

Nickname:

All About Her Clothes:

Personality:

Favorite Thing:

ABOUT THE AUTHOR & ARTIST

TOMOMI MIZUNA began her career as a freelance manga illustrator and writer after working for a game company. In addition to creating manga, she also designs for advertisements and children's books. Visit her website at www.mizutomo.com.